LIBERACE

T&J

Published by TAJ Books International LLC 2014
5501 Kincross Lane
Charlotte, North Carolina, USA
28277

www.tajbooks.com
www.tajminibooks.com

All notations of errors or omissions (author inquiries, permissions) concerning the content of this book should be addressed to info@tajbooks.com.

The Publisher would like to thank the Everett Collection, Allan Warren, Los Angeles Philharmonic Archives and Bob Thomas.

ISBN 978-1-84406-268-3 Hardback
978-1-62732-003-0 Paperback

Printed in China

1 2 3 4 5 18 17 16 15 14

LIBERACE

T&J

ISABELLA ALSTON

LIBERACE

W ladziu Valentino Liberace was born May 16, 1919, in West Allis, Wisconsin. He had a twin sibling who died in childbirth, but Wladziu was a healthy baby boy. His mother, Frances Zuchowska, knew the moment she laid eyes on her son that he would be destined for greatness, not only because of his robust health and full 13 pounds, but because he was born with a caul (a harmless membrane covering his face and head). The presence of a caul occurs in roughly one in 80,000 births and has been viewed since medieval times as a sign of good fortune and luck for the child.

Wladziu's father, Salvatore (which he later changed to Sam because it was easier to pronounce) Liberace, was an Italian immigrant, originally from Formia, Italy. Wladziu's mother was of Polish descent. Frances chose the name Valentino because of her fondness for the actor Rudolph Valentino. Wanting to represent her Polish origins, she chose the name Wladziu (the Polish version of Walter), which Liberace's father abhorred. Later on in life, when his career began to take off, Liberace legally dropped his first and middle names to be known solely by his (now famous) surname. Liberace was one of first entertainers to be known by a single name, an occurrence that is quite prevalent today.

Salvatore was a musician, and the earliest musical influence in Liberace's life. He immigrated to America as a young man, in search of the quintessential American Dream, which he would not find but his son did. Salvatore came from a large Italian family. He was able to study music and played the trumpet, clarinet, and French horn, the last being his instrument of choice. Before Salvatore left Italy, his older brother had made a similar move from their provincial Italian town to the bustling streets of Philadelphia, Pennsylvania. Salvatore's brother was a trombonist and was able to find numerous gigs in the States.

So Salvatore packed up his few possessions and boarded a boat destined for Ellis Island in 1906. At first, he found it more difficult than his brother to find employment, because typically only symphony orchestras and military bands

LIBERACE

featured French horns. Despite this initial setback, he was able to secure a position in John Philip Sousa's band, with which he toured the United States for a brief period. After this initial stint, Salvatore made ends meet by traveling around with his horn, finding jobs wherever he could.

During his itinerant period, Salvatore met his future wife and the mother of Liberace, Frances Zuchowska. She was a young, modest Polish girl who came from a family of farmers. Salvatore's Italian charm and artistic flair were both enchanting and mysterious to the rather innocent Frances, who fell in love with him instantly. They married and then moved back to Philadelphia. Two years later, their first son, George, was born.

The honeymoon did not last long and soon the couple was bickering over where to live. Frances disliked the hustle and bustle of a metropolitan city like Philadelphia, but Salvatore was strongly opposed to this idea because his chances for employment were much greater in the city. He ultimately conceded to Frances' wishes, however, and the family moved

back to Wisconsin, settling in West Allis, the small Milwaukee suburb where Liberace would eventually be born.

West Allis was primarily a workers' town populated by immigrants. Luckily, Salvatore was able to land a job with a local band, the International Harvester Band, and played regularly at the Schlitz Palm Garden. The couple's second child, Angelina, was born in 1914. Five years later Frances give birth to Liberace and his still-born twin brother. Frances would frequently say to friends and family that Liberace "took all the strength" from his twin while in the womb and his energy in life was consistent with her theory.

Frances and Salvatore would always have a rocky relationship. Neighbors made note of many loud arguments in their house. These fights were primarily driven by Frances' arguing that Salvatore was not adequately providing for the family. Salvatore's pride kept him (initially) from seeking employment outside of the music industry, which was proving harder and harder to make a living from. But Salvatore blamed Frances for his inability

At the age of three holding a teddy bear, c. 1922

to find work as she had been so adamant about moving back to Wisconsin where jobs in the music industry were few and far between. Eventually, Salvatore bought a small grocery store in which they would both work. At night, Salvatore ventured into Milwaukee, hoping to make some extra money in the bars and nightclubs playing in the bands. The reality was that he did work very hard to try to provide for his family, although Frances was never happy, accusing him of cheating on her and neglecting both her and the children.

It would soon become apparent to Frances that her once robust son would grow into a fragile youth. Liberace was especially vulnerable to contracting pneumonia, to which he fell victim at least four times during his youth; the illness would later be the cause of his demise, a complication of AIDs. During his childhood, these frequent bouts of illness meant Liberace was forced to spend much time at home while recuperating. Because his mother and father were busy during the day with the grocery store they owned, the young Liberace spent the majority of his time with his sister, Angelina. They mostly occupied themselves by playing make-believe and dress up, influences that made themselves well known later in Liberace's professional and personal life in terms of his costumes and decorating style.

Salvatore ensured that all of his offspring were well educated in music and taught to play musical instruments, and Liberace's talent stood out at a young age. While Angelina struggled to memorize pieces on the piano, Liberace mastered them with an ease that far exceeded his four years of age, a feat that impressed both his parents and his instructors.

When Liberace was just seven years old, he memorized the full 17-page score of Mendelssohn's "Midsummer Night's Dream" within the short period of one day. Furthermore, Liberace decided to memorize this piece not because it was assigned to him, but because his sister (13 years old at the time) was expected to memorize it and found the piece too troublesome to remember. Situations like this were early signs that Liberace was destined for a significant musical career,

With his mother, Frances, whom he adored, 1954

thanks to his innate musical sensibilities. Liberace's youth was plagued by a speech impediment that was taken seriously by his father and teachers, who believed the cause might be physical, but his mother refused to acknowledge it was of any concern and insisted that Liberace was perfectly normal in every way except for his speech.

One day, Salvatore was discussing his son's speech problem with a fellow musician, Steve Swedish, who suggested that perhaps the speech impediment was caused by having too short of a lingual frenulum—the small piece of flesh that connects the bottom of the tongue to the area located behind the bottom, front teeth. This is actually a rare but recognized disorder referred to as ankyloglossia. Salvatore took this possibility to heart and decided to pursue it in case Liberace's speech impediment was a result of this condition.

So, a week later, Salvatore took Liberace to the doctor and had them cut this miniscule piece of flesh in half, hoping that the problem would be solved. Alas,

there was no change in Liberace's speech abilities. Thus, Swedish, Salvatore's musician friend, volunteered that since Liberace's speech impediment was obviously not a physical problem, it must be a mental one. He suggested that Salvatore take his young son to a speech therapist, mentioning that he knew of a good one, Father Hamilton. This marked the start of Liberace's seven-year stint in speech therapy, which he would eventually graduate from at the age of 14.

An album cover from recordings early in his career

A portrait in the early days of Liberace's career

LIBERACE

Father Hamilton's approach was to focus on the clear pronunciation of vowels. After this was mastered, Hamilton then began to work on forcing Liberace's learned Italian-American accent out of his repertoire. For example, hearing his father speak, Liberace pronounced the "th" sound as if it were a "d." By the time Liberace finished his seven years of therapy, his speech was close to perfect, almost too perfect and was something that critics would note in the years to come. Nevertheless, this very deliberate, clear pronunciation was one of Liberace's lasting trademarks, especially once he found success with television audiences.

Liberace performed regularly on television as the star of "The Liberace Show" from 1952 to 1955 and again in 1969.

At the piano with his mother and his brother George

LIBERACE

THE CONSERVATORY YEARS

About this time, Liberace was starting to outgrow his piano teacher and his father decided that if his son was to continue improving his natural talent, he must find him a better, more experienced instructor. He remembered a woman with whom he had played in a symphony. Her name was Florence Kelly and she was now a teacher at the Wisconsin College of Music. Salvatore thought it might be worth a shot to visit Ms. Kelly, so off they went to Milwaukee. Liberace played a few pieces for her. She was very impressed by the considerable talent he showed for a boy of such a young age. She agreed to take him on as a pupil and also managed to secure a scholarship for him with the conservatory.

Thanks to Florence Kelly, Liberace would become a skilled, disciplined, and creative pianist in the years to come. Both teacher and pupil were rather hardheaded and often found themselves in disputes and disagreements, although these spats were almost always short-lived and only helped to further define Liberace's character.

By 1929, when Liberace was 10 years old, his family was in rather undesirable financial straights—and they were not alone. This was the year of the worst stock market crash in U.S. history and marked the start of the Great Depression. Almost every single American citizen was hit hard by the country's dire economic situation.

Artists and musicians, such as Salvatore, were especially hard-pressed to find work in the midst of the very severe downturn in the economy. The film industry was transitioning from silent films to talkies, meaning that the once ubiquitous background orchestral music was no longer a necessity. Once, this had been a "go-to" job for Salvatore. In order to make ends meet, Frances was forced to get a job in a cookie factory, while George, Liberace's older brother, drove a grocery truck and taught piano lessons on the side. Liberace's sister, Angelina, found a job as a secretary as well as a nurse. Liberace was able to help by washing dishes in various restaurants, as well as by playing piano accompaniment for dance classes in the area. To strain the

An early Liberace, dressed to kill, at the piano. The candelabra is already a part of the act.

LIBERACE

family's finances even further, Frances had another child, a son named Rudolph, this year.

Although it was inevitable, Salvatore was greatly troubled by the fact that his wife and children now had to work in order to make ends meet. His Italian male pride was shattered in not being able to singlehandedly support his family. As a result, he turned to drinking in an attempt to drown his worries and his dependence on the bottle coincided with numerous extramarital affairs.

Salvatore eventually found work with Roosevelt's Works Progess Administration (WPA) Orchestra, which was notable as a major effort to help support America's unemployed artists. This job did not alone provide enough income to support the family, so Salvatore often worked in a factory by day when he could get the work although he never told his wife or children he had a day job too. Like many families during the Great Depression, a welfare check was needed to put enough food on the table each week and Frances heavily relied on it.

In later years, Liberace openly discussed this period as a regretful memory of his youth. He talked about how much he hated the family's lack of pretty much everything. This "shabbiness," as he characterized it, which he was forced to endure at such a young age, influenced his life thereafter. He described how he would walk 27 blocks and pay 15 cents to see a movie in a "clean, new" movie theater in lieu of walking just five blocks and paying only a nickel.

Liberace wasn't very popular at school, at least not at first. Many of the boys considered him to be a sissy. Despite this, his classmates recognized his talent and would pretty much use him as a provider of entertainment since he was always more than happy to play the piano whenever the opportunity arose. He refused to participate in any sports activities because he wanted to "save these hands."

He also played at dance studios during this period and he always opted for taking dance lessons, rather than receiving money, in exchange for playing. His

LIBERACE

natural rhythm meant that he picked up the moves rather fast. Perhaps his family would have preferred that he ditch the dance lessons and bring home the money instead.

This period also marked the first sign of his love for flamboyant costumes. His school had a "Character Day" once every year and Liberace always impressed his teachers and classmates. His most notable get-ups were Halle Selassie, Greta Garbo, and Yankee Doodle Dandy. Classmates later recalled that Liberace always made a concerted effort to be well-dressed, always wearing a coat and vest and even spats when the weather was colder. He also pioneered the first cooking class for boys at his high school. On the weekends, he would construct silk flower corsages which he would sell to the girls in his class for the dances.

While studying the classics with Ms. Kelly, the teenage Liberace played at local honky tonks and bars at night to earn a bit of extra money. These years followed the now outlawed prohibition era, so nightlife was thriving as Americans

frantically sought to relieve their pent-up demand for booze and unrelenting fun. When Frances found out the venues her son was performing in, she grounded him for a week. But Liberace did not let this stop him from making his engagements. One of his fellow bandmates would arrive at his window with a ladder and Liberace would sneak out to perform, his absence undetected by his mother.

The Basle Theater in Washington, Pennsylvania, Christmas 1955

Liberace in rhinestone bow tie and elaborate candelabra

19

LIBERACE

In general, Liberace was a very good student and son, except when these responsibilities interfered with his music. Despite his rowdy evening engagements, he continued to devote his days to practicing the classics. Frequenting these adult establishments in his teenage years meant that Liberace was introduced to booze and sex. His few encounters with alcohol ended rather badly—falling off the piano bench mid-song, for example—causing him to generally steer clear of alcohol in excessive amounts. He also lost his virginity to a blues singer during a brief affair with her. She was twice his age. Liberace later recalled that he was rather disappointed with his first sexual encounter, because he had wanted it to resemble more the idealized love scenes he had seen in films.

In June 1937, Liberace graduated from high school at the age of 18. Under his photograph in the yearbook was the rhyme: "Our Wally has already made his claim, with Paderewski, Gershwin, and others of fame." College was not an option for the young Liberace, not because he did not have sufficient grades

With Sammy Davis Jr., 1967, above, and with Elvis Presley, 1956, right

LIBERACE

to enroll, but because the cost of tuition was more than his family could afford. Furthermore, Liberace had no real interest in college, his number-one interest was music and that is what he lived and breathed.

One of Liberace's favorite pianists was performing at the Pabst Theater in Milwaukee. Not wanting to miss such a fabulous opportunity to see one of the "greats," he asked his father if he would like to accompany him to the show. Salvatore told him he couldn't because he had a rehearsal that night. Disappointed, but understanding of a fellow musician's need to rehearse with the band, he asked Ms. Kelly if she would attend the show with him, which she very happily agreed to do.

That evening, the two of them were giddy with excitement until Liberace spotted his father a few rows ahead of where they were seated. Salvatore was sitting next to an unfamiliar woman, leaning in much closer than a friend without romantic intentions would do. Liberace was devastated and his view of his father

was shattered. This night marked a very severe break in their relationship, one which would not be mended for many years. He never revealed what he saw to his mother, scared that she would suffer greatly at the news that his father truly was being unfaithful. Instead, he began to avoid both home and his father. The confusion and guilt he felt at keeping the secret would likely have destroyed him if he hadn't had his music as an outlet and escape.

For the next few years, Liberace continued to play music at bars and dance halls in the evenings, refining his art during the day. In 1939, Ms. Kelly suggested that he audition for a guest appearance in the Chicago Symphony. Ms. Kelly escorted him from Milwaukee to Chicago in the middle of a raging snow storm. By the time the pair arrived in Chicago, they were terribly worried that Liberace had missed his chance to audition. As luck would have it, one last individual was auditioning when they arrived. The man in charge of holding the auditions, Dr. Frederick Stock, was a stern and intimidating man who did

Figuratively "playing" his piano pool at his home in Sherman Oaks, CA, c. 1954

not hesitate to share his opinion of a performance. He barked the auditioning boy off the stage mid-song and ordered Liberace to begin his audition. To Liberace's surprise, Stock sat quietly throughout the entire audition, complimenting Liberace with a "well done" when he finished. Liberace won the position in the symphony.

During the six months in which he had to patiently wait for the symphony performance, Liberace adopted the name Walter Buster Keys to use for his local gigs in honky tonks and bars. This was done as a request from the symphony because it did not want Liberace to be associated with the popular music of the day lest it taint the symphony's classical image.

By 1941, Frances and Salvatore officially split. Two years later, Salvatore married Zona Smrz (the woman whom Liberace had caught him with a few years earlier at the Paderewski concert). At the same time Frances married an Italian named Alexander Casadonte. Neighbors speculated that Frances and Casadonte had been having a clandestine affair prior to her and Salvatore's divorce. Casadonte hailed from the same Italian village, Formia, as Salvatore and had briefly roomed with the Liberace family after immigrating to the United States.

With the break-up of his parents' marriage, Liberace ceased all communication with his father. The silence lasted for the next 12 years. The same year, 1941, also marked the start of WWII and the country began mobilizing for war. Liberace's elder brother, George, joined the Navy. Liberace was drafted, but did not qualify for service due to a back injury he had sustained in childhood. As a result, Liberace had even more time to focus on his music career.

Liberace expressed his concerns to Ms. Kelly regarding his inability to define his muscial style as either classical or pop. He truly loved both and had a reasonably successful career dabbling between the two musical genres, although he knew that he needed to settle with one so that he could have a definitive style. Kelly suggested a rather obvious, but novel

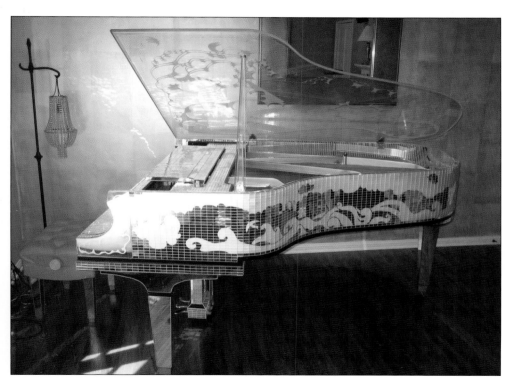

It is difficult to judge which was dearer to his heart—his pianos or his costumes—but both played second fiddle to making music for the masses who enthusiastically cheered his ostentatiousness.

LIBERACE

concept: combine the two! She urged him to venture beyond the confines of Milwaukee, Wisconsin, and look for something bigger and better. Thus, Liberace packed his things and headed for New York City, the city where dreams come true! Or, they can just as easily be crushed to smithereens, but at least the Big Apple offered much more opportunity for success than Milwaukee did.

THE BIG APPLE

Liberace's first gig was at a New Jersey hotspot called Pal's Cabin. The job offered steady employment and the locale was not quite as intimidating or threatening as the big city, allowing Liberace to establish himself before expanding his horizons to bigger and better gigs at a later date. In addition to the copious job opportunities and artistic inspiration found in New York City, the "city that never sleeps" also provided an anonymous environment in which Liberace was free to embrace his homosexuality. He could be accepted for who he was, not judged by others based on who they thought he should be.

He soon signed with an agent, Mae Johnston, who helped him land a gig at the Persian Room in the Plaza Hotel. He was hired as an intermission pianist, which rather disappointed the budding star, but he needed the money and welcomed just about any opportunity to entertain the public. Liberace was excited that the main act was a Milwaukeean named Hildegarde. He admired her deft performance and was captivated by her commanding presence. She is said to have advised him that he should never play an encore in order to leave the audience wanting more. The Plaza management ultimately fired him because they thought his habit of asking his audiences for requests was crossing the line away from sophisticated, mid-town entertainment appropriate to such a high-brow, white-shoe establishment.

His agent Johnston found him other work around Manhattan, mainly as a fill-in pianist between nightclub acts. Liberace also landed a few gigs at movie theaters, supper clubs, and stage shows. At this point, he was making

Taking the keys to one of his early automobile creations

about $175 per week. During one of his performances, he spotted Johnston in the audience accompanied by several men. She approached him after the show, explaining that the men with her were Music Corporation of America (MCA) executives who wanted him to assume the duties of one of their top-billed artists who was shipping off with the Navy and lead his orchestra. This was a stellar opportunity for the young musician, an opportunity that would provide him with instant fame and a significant pay increase.

But to the executives' and his agent's chagrin, Liberace passed on the offer because he was worried he would lose his unique identity if he stepped into the role of an already well-known musician. The result of snubbing his nose at the music industry executives was that suddenly jobs that he used to be offered in New York City began to disappear. His patience with this new big-city battle quickly ran out and he sought other paths. He remembered that Clarence Goodwin, a man he had met while playing a show in Boston, had extended an invitation for

With Mae West; they remained friends throughout their lives.

Liberace to stay with his wife and him if Liberace ever ventured out to Los Angeles. So, without further ado, Liberace headed to Los Angeles and greener pastures.

Man about town with Joanne Rio, 1954

LIBERACE

With Betty White

HOLLYWOOD

O nce again, Liberace packed his belongings and headed for the Pacific coast. Luckily the offer of a place to crash still stood and Liberace stayed with the Goodwins for an entire year. During that year, Goodwin encouraged Liberace to ditch Johnston and suggested that he replace her as his agent and manager. Liberace concurred and the deal was done. Goodwin was a wealthy and well-established member of the Los Angeles community and was able to get the word out about the new musician in town and create significant buzz about him. The stage was set for Liberace to dazzle audiences on the West Coast. The seeds of a lucrative career were sown.

Liberace's favorite place to go in Los Angeles was the Hollywood Piano Exchange, a piano store that specialized in catering to the film studios. Virtually any kind of piano from any era could be found in the store. Liberace fell in love with an enormous gilded piano he saw there. The uniqueness of the piano lay not only in its appearance but in the fact that

With the ice skater Sonja Henie at Mocambo Nightclub in 1955

With the ice skater Sonja Henie (left) and actress Susan Hayward in 1955

instead of three wires per note, as most pianos have, it had four; this fourth wire per note made a tremendous difference in the sound, similar to the sound of a church organ.

Liberace raved to Goodwin about the piano. Goodwin insisted that Liberace must have it if he felt so strongly about it. Liberace protested, but found the piano in the living room the next day. Goodwin explained that with such a grand piano, Liberace would draw larger crowds, and that larger crowds meant a bigger paycheck. A stunned Liberace listened as Goodwin argued that Liberace could easily pay him back for the piano. With World War II still on-going, manufacturing businesses were booming in Los Angeles and workers employed in the factories had the means and desire to frequent night clubs, providing Liberace an ample audience that appreciated his talents.

A publicity shot with Dorothy Malone, his co-star in the film Sincerely Yours, *1955*

With Delores Perry, 1958

LIBERACE

HIS STYLE EMERGES

A fter about a year in Los Angeles, Liberace felt it was time to return to New York and try again for the "big time." He had rebuilt his confidence and self-esteem, thanks to Goodwin's support as well as the positive reception he had received in California. He realized, however, that he needed to develop a style of performing that was uniquely his or he would risk being swept up into the crowd of aspiring musicians who were constantly seeking success in the big city. He needed to stand out from the rest, and he decided that in order to do this he would take the familiar, but rework it for modern audiences.

He began by selecting popular works from the greats like Paderewski, Horowitz, and Rubenstein, practicing the pieces for about 12 hours each day so that he could perfect the timing of his playing to perfectly coincide with the tracks. Rather than playing the pieces in their (often lengthy) entirety, he shortened them to their most essential parts, realizing that audiences were now exhibiting shorter attention spans and were looking for entertainment, not art. He may have even come up with one of the first surround sound stereo systems, placing speakers around the room so that the recording sounded as "live" as possible.

He took his act to the Persian Room at the Plaza. The management liked it and hired him straight away at a high salary. He had succeeded in elevating his act, leaving behind the job of intermission pianist. His act now followed his friend Hildegarde's. His was now the showcased act. It was at this time that he added his signature candelabra atop his piano, feeling that it created a special ambience and elegance.

The first show at the Persian Room was a complete smash hit! Liberace knew how to charm and work his audience by engaging them and telling jokes or small anecdotal stories at appropriate points during the show. They begged for an encore, though he took Hildegarde's advice and politely refused, knowing that they would then want to come back for more. A reviewer of the show said that Liberace appeared

With Rosemary Clooney

LIBERACE

to be a cross between Cary Grant and Robert Alda. The reviewer raved about his mannerisms and showmanship on stage. For a New York review, this was great news for Liberace!

Such success from his newly adopted performance style led to him being invited to play a Liszt concerto at the New Jersey Symphony, as well as a gig as a soloist on a popular radio show of the day. He was an exceptional self-promoter, sending postcards to potential employers every time he had a successful show—which was always! This tactic landed him a job in Las Vegas in the Ramona Room at the Last Frontier casino and hotel.

HELLO, LAS VEGAS!

Liberace was shocked by the overall kitsch of the hotel and casino, especially that the performers had to make their entrances winding through the tables on the dining room floor, greeting diners as they passed. Before offering him the job, the hotel's manager had asked him what his current salary was. Liberace lied and told them he was being paid $750 a week,

when in reality he was really only making $350. Imagine his surprise when upon his arrival in Las Vegas, he was informed that the hotel's management felt $750 was too little and that they would be redrafting his contract in order to pay him a whopping $1,500 a week. One funny story from his first rehearsal at the Ramona Room involved him naively mistaking Howard Hughes for the lighting technician.

In 1945, Liberace's older brother, George, was back in the states after serving four years in the Navy. Liberace suggested that he join him as his manager. His booking manager, MCA, did their job quite well but he really needed someone he could trust and rely on to help him manage more mundane issues such as publicity, technical issues, and general managerial duties.

Frances was extremely supportive of the idea, because she was constantly concerned with Liberace being alone out in the corrupt world. She believed that George would help keep her middle son grounded. George had aspired to be a musician, but he was now beginning to

With Maureen O'Hara in 1957 in court during Liberace's
$25 million libel suit against Confidential *magazine*

LIBERACE

realize that he lacked the necessary talent and perhaps the closest he would come to musical fame was by helping his baby brother.

The duo made a good pair: Liberace was the flamboyant, creative, excitable one, whereas George made sure they stayed on schedule, paid bills, and never got too carried away in frivolities. Furthermore, George had sound knowledge of how the music business worked, which helped out immensely. In many ways, Liberace looked upon George as a sort of surrogate father figure, since his own father had been absent for much of his youth.

The brothers rarely quarreled, although the one issue that caused significant tension between the two was Liberace's tendency for extravagance. George felt anything that was more than was necessary was unnecessary; he did not understand the power of bling when it comes to showmanship and performing. Liberace certainly had enough knowledge of bling for the two of them. He often enthused that "Too much of a good thing is wonderful!"

Liberace had such success at the Ramona Room, he was signed to a 10-year contract with the Last Frontier hotel and casino in 1947. The contract stipulated that he was obligated to play a certain number of shows each year during the 10-year period. At one of the shows, Liberace had a chance encounter with the infamous gangster Bugsy Siegel.

Siegel approached Liberace in the lobby after the performance, gruffly informing him that his act was too classy for this "dump" and urged him to appear at Siegel's own resort down the road, the Flamingo. Not wanting to get involved with the mob, he told Siegel he would think about it and fretted over what to do for several days. He went to his manager at the Last Frontier for advice, and she informed him that the decision was his. Luckily for Liberace, he never had to decide. Siegel was assassinated a couple of months later by an unknown gunman.

LIBERACE

MOVIES AND TELEVISION

Things were really starting to take off for Liberace; he even received an invitation to play for President Truman at the White House News Photographers Association dinner at the Statler Hotel in Washington, DC, in 1950. Afterward, when asked about the experience, Liberace vividly recalled the numerous guidelines set forth by the Secret Service regarding his characteristic repartee with which he enlivened his performance. To name just a few of the prohibitions, Truman's security detail stipulated that Liberace was not to refer in any way to Truman's recent Florida vacation or the "controversial pictures of him in bathing trunks" and that Liberace's remarks should be directed to the audience and not to the President because he was a modest man.

Liberace displayed his typical confidence in his artistic talent and demeanor, however, cracking jokes throughout the performance and requesting audience participation for specific numbers. After the show, Truman, himself a rather accomplished pianist, thanked Liberace and invited him to perform at the White House once the on-going major renovation was completed (no social events could be held at the White House from late 1948 until early 1952) because he thought his wife and daughter would greatly enjoy his show. Liberace never did return to the Truman White House for the promised follow-up performance.

One of the more prominent figures at the White House News Photographers Association dinner in Washington was Nate Blumberg, the president of Universal-International Pictures. Upon his return to New York City, he immediately contacted the studio executives and urged them to get Liberace signed up ASAP for a screen test. That evening at Liberace's show at the Mocambo, a hoard of Universal executives showed up to view this new name. They unanimously agreed that he was a promising young artist and decided to cast him in their upcoming film *East of Java* (later changed to *South Sea Sinner*) released in 1950.

The film was primarily being used as a tool to promote Universal's new blonde bombshell, Shelley Winters. The

President Truman (center) with Liberace (second from right) and other entertainers at the 1950 White House News Photographers Association Dinner at the Statler Hotel, Washington, DC.

With his mother, Frances

An evening out in the company of two legendary actresses and singers,
Judy Garland (middle) and Sophie Tucker (right)

LIBERACE

plot wasn't anything too original. A handsome man is stranded on an island in the Pacific. The handsome man falls for the sexy piano bar singer (Winters), who is unfortunately involved in a sticky situation with the bar owner, thus dragging the handsome man into the messy problem along with her.

Liberace was, not surprisingly, cast as the pianist in the film. On first introduction, Liberace was rather intimidated by Ms. Winters because of her very direct approach to personal communication and rarely censored herself. The two would eventually become friends though, thanks to their shared difficulties with insomnia and love for hot fudge sundaes.

The film did not get great reviews and Ms. Winters was dubbed "the poor man's Mae West," whereas Liberace received generally positive reviews from the critics. But certainly his role couldn't have been too much of a challenge since he was basically playing himself, pounding out tunes on the piano keyboard.

With the income he made from the film, Liberace bought a modest house on Camellia Street in North Hollywood. He immediately telephoned his mother in Milwaukee and asked her to sell the small ice cream store she was running and move out to California to live with him. Frances was at first a bit unsure of what to do. Until this moment, she had lived the majority of her adult life in Milwaukee and had planned to retire there, the place she felt was truly home.

But once the initial shock wore off, Frances warmed to the idea and happily moved to the West Coast to live with her increasingly famous son and to be closer to her eldest son, George. Her second husband had passed away in 1945 and her only daughter, Angelina, was married with children of her own. Her youngest son, Rudolph, was busy with his own life. Making up her mind that there really was nothing left for her in Wisconsin, Frances sold the ice cream shop within a week and headed out to join her beloved son, Liberace.

By now, Liberace was almost 30 years old. He was extremely successful, earning

Barry Langford with Liberace in the Langford Silver Shop in London in the 1960s; Langford was a TV and music director/producer in the 1960s and 1970s.

LIBERACE

White tie and tails, tuxedos, sequins—the more the merrier! And don't forget the candelabra and the rhinestone piano! Liberace was instantly recognizable on his album covers, which emulated his unique style.

A publicity photo from 1964

49

LIBERACE

about $3,000 a week. Despite his material success, he felt somewhat empty on the inside. For the large part, this sense of dissatisfaction stemmed from an inability to emotionally reach the public to the extent that he desired with his music. Initially, he had anticipated that *South Seas Sinner* would rocket him into the realm of stardom, but the movie had been a disappointing flop.

About this time, Liberace was doing much soul searching, often coming dangerously close to giving up on his dream of being an all-star entertainer known the world over. In the midst of seeking his life's path, Liberace discovered a book by Claude M. Bristol that provided answers and guidance that spoke to his discontent. Bristol had made his money in the newspaper industry and was also a World War I veteran. Synthesizing the lessons learned from these two very challenging life paths resulted in insights that he used to devise a self-help technique. He published the elements of his technique in what was likely one of the first-ever self-help guides. The book was titled *The Magic of Believing*. Liberace devoured

Bristol's book, finally feeling as though someone else understood his approach to living. For the rest of his life, he lived by the words of this book, just as if it were the Bible.

Liberace lived and died by the following tenants:

To experience happiness, one must express happiness.

To find love, one must give love.

To possess wealth, one must value wealth.

To acquire health, one must live health.

To attain success, one must positively think success.

His dressing rooms and homes were filled with mirrors. Vanity was not the only reason; he truly believed (as did Bristol) that one should constantly reinforce themselves in their ability to succeed. The mirrors literally helped him to see himself and to visualize his own heady success.

With Ray Charles on "The Dinah Shore Show"
in 1963

LIBERACE

The majority of Liberace's thoughts were focused on how he could further promote himself and garner greater fame. After reading the book by Bristol, as well as evaluating his situation, he came to the conclusion that he would need to find a better manager than his brother George if he were to attain the level of success he so hoped to achieve. George was great when it came to getting the daily tasks done, but he was not an individual who looked ahead and "made big plans," the type of personality that Liberace thought his manager should have.

Careful not to hurt George's feelings, Liberace told George that he needed him to devote all of his time to conducting the orchestra, choosing the musical arrangements, and focusing his management skills solely on the musical aspect of his career. To Liberace's great relief, George responded to this new

The photographs on pages 53, 55, 57, 59, and 62–63 are by Allen Warren.

1968

request with great enthusiasm. He was naturally more inclined to succeed in the music world than in the business world; he just wasn't flexible enough as a thinker to be successful when it came to business dealings.

Once the whole George situation was settled, Liberace turned his attention to trying to find a suitable managerial firm that would be able to take him in the direction he wanted to go. The firm that kept bubbling to the top of conversation whenever artistic management was mentioned was the firm of Gabbe, Lutz, and Heller in Hollywood. Liberace encouraged George to use his tried-and-true tactic of sending post cards, which regaled the receiver of the success of recent Liberace shows, to the entertainment management firm.

Eventually, George simply walked into the offices of Gabbe, Lutz, and Heller. There he was greeted with "So you are the one who has been sending us all these postcards!" George informed them that he was in fact that man and asked them to come to the Orpheum Theater in downtown Los Angeles where they could witness Liberace's talent for themselves.

Sam Lutz and Seymour Heller agreed to attend but were initially unpersuaded by Liberace's performance. Liberace blamed the vastness of the performance space as well as the unimpressive audience as having been a deterrent to the enthusiasm of the two talent agents. George tried his best to make excuses as to why the performance fell short that day, but nothing worked to convince the two agents that they should consider representing Liberace.

Referring to what he had learned from Bristol's book, Liberace smiled at the two men and informed them that it was fine and maybe they would reconsider one day. A little less than a month after the disappointing performance, George returned to the offices of Gabbe, Lutz, and Heller to solicit his brother's show at the Hotel Del Coronado in San Diego. Both George and Liberace knew that the Del Coronado's venue would be much more suited to a successful performance and hoped that the agents would give

1968

LIBERACE

Liberace a second chance. To George's great surprise, Lutz and Heller informed him that they were already planning to see the show. After this performance, Liberace was accepted for representation by the firm.

Liberace's relationship with Lutz and Heller may be one of the best career moves he ever made. The team represented him from 1950 until his death in 1987. Recognizing that the new medium of television was the future of entertainment, the agents began to strategize how they could best present Liberace to a television audience. A break into television meant that Liberace would finally be able to reach the large audience he had always hoped for.

Liberace had already made several appearances on television, although most directors felt that a pianist was not captivating enough to warrant such a broad audience. In order to create a more interesting scene for the viewers, various directors panned through a sea of instruments and even included a cast of ballet dancers to accompany

Liberace's performance. The main issue, according to directors, was that the piano didn't provide enough movement to be captivating to the viewers at home.

But Liberace realized before anyone else that television was just the medium he needed for his act. He knew that his personality was the most captivating and charming in one-on-one situations, which the medium of television closely emulated. He rememberd, for example, that his initial audition with his agents Lutz and Heller flopped because the performance space was so vast, destroying the sense of intimacy that he strove to create with his audience.

Lutz and Heller agreed with Liberace that he needed to break into television and contacted Don Fedderson, the general manager of the local Los Angeles Channel 13 station. Fedderson was familiar with Liberace and thought he was very talented. But just to be sure, he attended one of Liberace's performances at the Del Coronado Hotel and was not disappointed. He agreed Liberace had great potential for success on the new medium of television.

LIBERACE

Liberace was elated that he had so much support and happily anticipated the new direction his career was headed. In his shows, he played both the classics and popular music, always condensing the longer songs down to their essentials in an effort not to lose the audience's interest. Despite the strong support he was getting for his new television show, he was also faced with an equal amount of naysayers. Fedderson explained to Liberace that he needed to be sure to play for the "regular Joe" and not to the fancy snobs in Beverly Hills and New York City. This admonition was based on the fact that the "John and Jane Smiths" of the world were the primary viewers of primetime television.

Fedderson was extremely helpful to Liberace in his early tenure on television. He was able to critique Liberace's image and help hone his character to the ideal television personality. Already an extremely talented pianist and musician, Liberace knew that what mattered most in this forum was perfecting the performance side of his act.

Fedderson strongly emphasized the need to win over the audience, not simply attract them. He also instructed Liberace to get some cosmetic dental work done. Appearing on television meant that Liberace would often be shown in a close-up of his face and his uneven teeth could no longer afford to be ignored—regardless of how charmingly he smiled. So Liberace had his teeth capped. Fedderson also noted that audiences commented that Liberace was perceived as young and sophomoric. To help counter this impression, Liberace began to spray gray around his temples. He was wise to the fact that the bulk of his fan base was older women and he sought to appeal to their sensibilities.

"The Liberace Show" first aired in 1952 with little notice by the public. It would run until 1955 and then again in 1969. Most reviewers simply skimmed over it. Liberace was only making $1,000 per show in the early days out of which he had to pay George and the orchestra. This initial stagnant period wouldn't last for long, and soon the public was

1968

LIBERACE

raving about "that crazy Liberace!" Fedderson had the novel idea that the Citizens National Trust and Savings Bank should sponsor the new hit show. Liberace announced on national television that anyone who opened an account at the bank with a minimum of $10 would receive a complimentary Liberace record. Three months later the bank had a whopping $600,000 in new accounts, simply because of Liberace and Fedderson's promotional tactic.

Liberace was so popular, in fact, that when he advertised canned crab meat on his show, the manufacturer immediately sold out of its entire supply, even in a place like Corpus Christi, Texas, where fresh crab meat is available about 10 months out of the year.

Only a year after "The Liberace Show" first aired, 100 television stations nationwide were broadcasting it. This outnumbered the amount of stations that carried the hit sitcom "I Love Lucy." Liberace worked tirelessly to keep the show fresh and exciting. For example, for his popular number "Kitten on the Keys,"

the producers went so far as to bring in a live cat to walk across the piano in mid-song.

One day, Liberace noticed a nun in the studio audience and asked her if she would come up on stage to kneel and pray while he played "Ave Maria" on the piano. Liberace never underestimated the power of props in his show—and boy was the nun the real thing! Another unique touch was that his mother was always sitting in the front row for every show. Liberace never failed to introduce her, making her presence known to the world.

In 1952, he played the Hollywood Bowl, an open air theater nestled in the Hollywood Hills. In an attempt to stand out from the crowd—and to be seen on the stage in the low lighting of the bowl—Liberace and Fedderson decided that Liberace should perform dressed in white tie and tails. This marked the beginning of Liberace's habitually dressing in flamboyant costumes that grew ever more elaborate as the years passed. Critics did not initially respond well to this new look, but the saying "any press

1968

LIBERACE

is good press" seems to tell the tale. In remembering Liberace today, his costumes are inseparable from his personality as a performer and in no way detract from his genius on the piano. The combination of glitz and virtuosity at the keyboard inspired and influenced many celebrities, but none as much as the indomitable powerhouse known as Elton John.

Liberace was invited back twice to Washington, DC, to perform for President Eisenhower, once again at the White House Photographers Association Dinner. Just a few months later, he headlined at Carnegie Hall in New York City. He was also frequently employed by various members of the Manhattan elite to play at their private parties.

As a general rule, critics would never be great fans of Liberace. Some felt that he focused far too much on the fanciful "extras" in his musical delivery rather than on showcasing his innate and unquestionable talent. These negative reviews would hurt his pride to a certain degree, but he nevertheless brushed himself off and continued on his way.

Early in life, he had learned to counter negativity via the use of humor, which is the tactic he would continue to use throughout his career. His humor was patently obvious in his performances—an intrinsic element that audiences adored.

Despite being a homosexual (albeit unacknowledged) and an exuberant, if controversial, performer, Liberace always upheld his strict Catholic beliefs instilled in him by his mother. He was also a staunch conservative when it came to

Liberace's house in Palm Springs, California, where one of his seven dining rooms (see opposite page!) could be found.

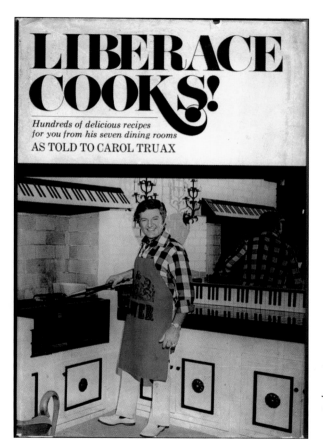

A 1970 cookbook published by Doubleday and Company featured recipes from Liberace's seven dining rooms.

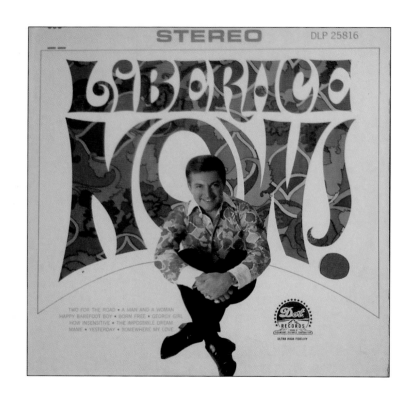

LIBERACE

politics and fervently disagreed with rebellion of any sort against established government, particularly the anti-war demonstrations of the 1960s. In keeping with his innate conservatism he was a strong believer in the benefits of a free market and capitalism.

For a working-class, first-generation American immigrant, the fame and success Liberace achieved was an excellent example to countless others with the same background as to what hard work could achieve in America. Because he hailed from such modest origins, he was able to appeal to the general populace, the "Jane and John Smiths" of the world who were his main audience, and was not perceived by them as snobbish or arrogant regardless of his grandiose appearance and lifestyle. His fan base, largely middle-aged to elderly women, inundated him with roughly 10,000 letters a week.

As often occurs in cases of sudden fame and wealth, Liberace spent his income extravagantly and with abandon. The architectural design of the first house he

built in Los Angeles drew pervasively on the piano as a theme throughout. The piano theme even extended to a piano-shaped swimming pool. He would gradually add homes in Palm Springs and Las Vegas, each more ostentatiously decorated than the last.

Observing how well his first television promotional stint with the bank had turned out, Liberace exploited his persuasive abilities by endorsing numerous businesses over the years that sought his unique appeal in their advertising campaigns. In doing so he padded their pockets as well as his. The demand for his sponsorship was also compensated with the goods that he hawked. Cadillac, for example, sent him a white sedan.

For someone who pretty much came from nothing and grew up in the Great Depression, all of his new-found money and fame seemed too good to be true. He truly enjoyed it! He never developed much control over his spending and was very generous with his friends, family, and lovers.

Sharing the piano with the Muppets, 1978

LIBERACE

Gossip columnists were constantly referring (although mostly tongue in cheek) to Liberace's blatant homosexual tendencies. In 1956, he sued the U.K.'s *Daily Mirror* for libel, appearing in court to testify that he was not a homosexual and had never partaken in any sort of homosexual acts. He ultimately won the law suit, gaining an 8,000 pound sterling settlement from the magazine. He told reporters after the trial that he "cried all the way to the bank!" A year later, he sued the American gossip magazine *Confidential* for the same reason.

By now, the rumor that Liberace preferred boys to girls was a frequent topic for Hollywood gossip columnists. He made the front page of *Confidential* in 1957 with the headline: "Why Liberace's Theme Song Should Be 'Mad about the Boy!'" For the most part, the subject remained in the realm of rumor and gossip until later in Liberace's life.

In 1956, Liberace traveled to Havana, Cuba, to play a show, followed by a European tour during which he met Pope Pius XII, a memory he often referred to as "the highlight of his life." Just four years later he was invited to perform in London with Nat King Cole and Sammy Davis Jr., an offer he readily accepted.

Life is composed of both the good and the bad, and Liberace's life was not unusual in that regard. On July 19, 1957, his mother Frances was attacked by two masked men in the garage of their home at 15405 Valley Vista Boulevard in Sherman Oaks, California. Liberace was on a European tour, performing at the Moulin Rouge night club in Paris, France, when the attack occurred. Not until he finished the show was he told about the break-in. The attack happened just a few hours after Liberace's deposition in his $25 million libel suit against *Confidential* magazine, which had made allegations that he was a homosexual, a charge he fought and won, even if the reality was that the magazine was correct in its assertions of his sexual orientation.

Frances was not badly hurt, thanks perhaps to a stiff corset she was wearing, but because Liberace's attachment to his mother was so strong, his retinue did

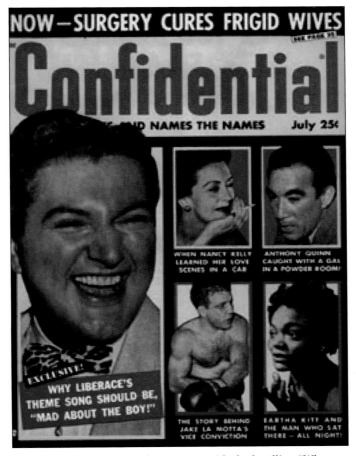

Confidential *cover, July 2, 1957, with the headline "Why Liberace's Theme Song Should Be 'Mad About the Boy!'"*

LIBERACE

not want to risk telling him before the show in case it negatively impacted his performance. From then on, Liberace had armed guards patrolling his properties as well as his brothers' houses.

In 1963, Liberace became very sick with renal (kidney) failure, a side effect of being overwhelmed by the dry cleaning fumes emitted by his numerous newly laundered costumes stored in his small dressing room. Doctors informed him that his illness was so severe it was fatal, so he wasted no time in spending his fortunes on pretty much anything and everything imaginable. Oddly enough, only a month later he was fully recovered.

This stroke of good—actually great—fortune gave him a much needed boost of energy. He returned to Las Vegas and amped up his act a few more notches. He referred to himself as "Mr. Showmanship," "Glitter Man," and "One-Man Disneyland." His shows were more spectacular than ever; he even descended to the stage one evening hanging by an invisible wire. His costumes were adorned from head to toe with ostrich feathers,

mink fur, jewels, sequins, and anything that shone or was ridiculously excessive. His shows included chorus girls, animals, and even cars. He was actually driven onto the stage by a chauffeur in one of his many cars that he made a part of his show. He took costuming and props further than most and it paid off in spades with his audiences.

1983

Two portraits at Liberace's home, Los Angeles, 1974, above and right

LIBERACE

Liberace did quite a lot to help Barbra Streisand get a leg up in the music industry. From July 2 to August 4, 1963, Barbra opened his show at the Riviera hotel in Las Vegas. She sang a duet with him in one of her first big show business breaks. Her Brooklyn persona was not initially a hit with Liberace's fans but he threw all his chutzpah and energy into building her up as his new "discovery" and she won over the decidedly not-so-sophisticated, non–New York Las Vegas crowd.

In addition to his own television show, Liberace made frequent appearances on the most popular shows of the 1960s such as "The Ed Sullivan Show" and "The Tonight Show" with Jack Paar. He received a star on the Hollywood Walk of Fame in recognition of his outstanding contributions to the television industry. He even had a cameo appearance in a 1966 episode of "Batman," making the episode one of the highest-rated shows in the series' history.

In addition to his life as a performer, Liberace undertook several business endeavors. He owned an Italian restaurant in Las Vegas called Liberace's Tivoli Gardens and authored a cookbook, having had an affinity for cooking and eating from an early age, as well as a coffee table book about his life.

In the 1970s and early 1980s, Liberace was booked steadily for live shows at the Las Vegas Hilton and Lake Tahoe, earning $300,000 a week. His last performance was November 2, 1986, at New York's Radio City Music Hall. The 21-day appearance grossed $2.5 million. He died three months later on February 4, 1987, from cytomegalovirus (CMV) pneumonia resulting from acquired immunodeficiency syndrome (AIDS).

With Barbra Streisand in Las Vegas, 1963

LIBERACE

With actress Kristy McNichol, a friend of Liberace's niece Ina Liberace

At his home with the television interviewer Robin Leach

LIBERACE

BEHIND THE CANDELABRA

No book about Liberace in 2014 would be complete without a mention of the relationship Liberace had with Scott Thorson. *Behind the Candelabra: My Life with Liberace* is Thorson's account of their years together. Because the book was written after Liberace's death and because Liberace was silent on the issue in the last years of his life, Liberace's side of the story will never be known.

After five years together, in 1986 Liberace's former chauffeur (as part of his Las Vegas shows) and lover Scott Thorson filed a lawsuit against the aging star for $113 million. Thorson had been introduced to Liberace, 48 years his senior, in 1976 as a teenager.

Liberace hired Thorson to be his "personal friend and companion." According to Thorson, this meant a romantic relationship between the two. Liberace spent much money on the young Thorson taking him on exotic vacations, showering him with furs and jewelry, and according to Thorson, an orphan for much of his life, promising to adopt and care for him for the remainder of his life.

Thorson claimed that their relationship eventually disintegrated as a result of Liberace's blatant promiscuity and Thorson's own worsening drug addiction. He believes that this addiction was fueled by his plastic surgeon at the time, who provided him with a dangerous cocktail of meds that included cocaine, quaaludes, biphetamines, and Demerol. According to Thorson, his rather extensive cosmetic surgeries were at the behest of Liberace so that Thorson would resemble Liberace.

Thorson's legal action against Liberace was the first same-sex palimony law suit filed in the United States, justified according to Thorson because the two were in a committed relationship and lived together for several years. Four years after bringing the suit against Liberace, the pair reportedly agreed to settle out of court for the sum of $95,000, as well as three cars and two pet dogs (which the couple had previously shared).

The restaurant was opened by Liberace, who owned the entire shopping center, in 1983.
The Carluccio family bought it in 1988. It closed in 2011.

LIBERACE

HIS LEGACY

Almost a decade before his death on February 4, 1987, at the age of 67, Liberace opened a museum in Las Vegas—his performing home for many years—dedicated to whom other than himself. Housing all of his flamboyant outfits, pianos, cars, and jewelry, the Liberace Museum became a prominent attraction for Las Vegas tourists who were die-hard fans more than willing to venture away from the strip of casinos, nightclubs, and performance spaces to revel at the extravagant accoutrements of the world-famous entertainer's life, both on stage and off. With time, however, the museum's draw significantly diminished, forcing it to closed its doors in October 2010.

Visitors to the museum were welcomed with the following quote: "This is the story of a poor Wisconsin boy, son of European immigrants, who through his great musical talent and fabulous personality became an icon of show business and the epitome of the American dream."

In August 2013, Liberace's 15,000-square-foot Las Vegas mansion was sold for $500,000 in cash, $3 million less than what it changed hands for seven years earlier. Martyn Ravenhill, the British businessman who bought the house, claims he was inspired to learn to play the piano after experiencing Liberace's talent. Now he owns the two-bedroom, ten-bathroom home once decorated so lavishly, and some would say garishly, with gilt statues and velvet settees that enthralled, inspired, and defined the entertainer.

The chandeliers, mirrored bar, and piano-key floor tiles still adorn the house, the very same house that witnessed much of the five-year clandestine (at least to the public) affair between Scott Thorson and Liberace, whom Scott called Lee. Their story (from Scott Thorson's point of view) was recently recounted in the HBO movie *Behind the Candelabra*. Michael Douglas won acclaim for his portrayal of Liberace as did Matt Damon for his performance in the role of Scott Thorson.

On stage in Las Vegas with his famous rhinestone piano

LIBERACE

Liberace opened the museum in Las Vegas on April 15, 1979. It closed in 2010. His brother George was the director.

An early-1980s Christmas costume that Liberace wore for performances at the Las Vegas Hilton and at Radio City Music Hall in New York City. It was designed by Michael Travis, with fur design by Anna Nateece. It is one of many that was displayed at the now-closed Liberace Museum.

A small sampling of Liberace's one-of-a-kind automobiles displayed at the Liberace Museum; on the right is the mirrored Rolls Royce that matched several of his mirrored pianos, which co-starred with Liberace in his Las Vegas show.

One of Liberace's many pianos and candelabras at the
Liberace Museum in Las Vegas

The fully developed Liberace persona by the end of his career

Liberace's tomb at Forest Lawn in Hollywood Hills

LIBERACE, ARRIVEDERCI

87-022886	CERTIFICATE OF DEATH	3Ø 000766

STATE FILE NUMBER
STATE OF CALIFORNIA

1A NAME OF DECEDENT First	1B Middle	1C Last
		LIBERACE

3 SEX	4 RACE/ETHNICITY	5 SPANISH/HISPANIC	6 DATE OF BIRTH	1D DATE OF DEATH MONTH DAY YEAR	2B HOUR
Male	Polish- White/Italian	NO	May 16, 1919	February 4, 1987	1405

7 AGE		
67 YEARS		

DECEDENT PERSONAL DATA

8 BIRTHPLACE OF DECEDENT (STATE OR FOREIGN COUNTRY)	9 NAME AND BIRTHPLACE OF FATHER	10 BIRTH NAME AND BIRTHPLACE OF MOTHER
Wisconsin	Salvatore Liberace - Italy	Frances Zuchowski - Wisconsin

11A CITIZEN OF WHAT COUNTRY	11B IF DECEASED WAS EVER IN MILITARY GIVE DATES OF SERVICE	12 SOCIAL SECURITY NUMBER	13 MARITAL STATUS	14 NAME OF SURVIVING SPOUSE or WIFE, ENTER BIRTH NAME
USA	19 TO 19	472-14-4916	Never Married	

15 PRIMARY OCCUPATION	16 NUMBER OF YEARS THIS OCCUPATION	17 EMPLOYER IF SELF EMPLOYED, SO STATE	18 KIND OF INDUSTRY OR BUSINESS
Entertainer/Pianist	42	Self-employed	Entertainment

USUAL RESIDENCE

19A USUAL RESIDENCE — STREET ADDRESS (STREET AND NUMBER OR LOCATION)	19B	19C CITY OR TOWN
4982 Shirley Street	198	Las Vegas

19D COUNTY	19E STATE
Clark	Nevada

1 OF 2

20 NAME AND ADDRESS OF INFORMANT RELATIONSHIP
Mr. Joel R. Strote, executor & truste

PLACE OF DEATH

21A PLACE OF DEATH	21B COUNTY
Residence	Riverside

21C STREET ADDRESS (STREET AND NUMBER OR LOCATION)	21D CITY OR TOWN
226 Alejo Road	Palm Springs

280 South Beverly Drive
Beverly Hills, California 90212

CAUSE OF DEATH

22 DEATH WAS CAUSED BY (ENTER ONLY ONE CAUSE PER LINE FOR A, B AND C) IMMEDIATE CAUSE		24 WAS DEATH REPORTED TO CORONER?
CONDITIONS, IF ANY (A) Pending DUE TO, OR AS A CONSEQUENCE OF		Yes 60121
WHICH GAVE RISE TO THE IMMEDIATE CAUSE (B) DUE TO, OR AS A CONSEQUENCE OF		25 WAS BIOPSY PERFORMED?
STATING THE UNDERLYING CAUSE LAST (C) 19:55, 6 II 87		No
		26 WAS AUTOPSY PERFORMED? Yes

23 OTHER SIGNIFICANT CONDITIONS— CONTRIBUTING TO DEATH BUT NOT RELATED TO CAUSE GIVEN IN 22A	27 WAS OPERATION PERFORMED FOR ANY CONDITION IN ITEMS 22 OR 23? TYPE OF OPERATION DATE

PHYSICIAN'S CERTIFICATION

28A I CERTIFY THAT DEATH OCCURRED AT THE HOUR, DATE AND PLACE STATED FROM THE CAUSES STATED I ATTENDED DECEDENT SINCE I LAST SAW DECEDENT ALIVE (ENTER MO. DA. YR.) (ENTER MO. DA. YR.)	28B PHYSICIAN— SIGNATURE AND DEGREE OR TITLE	28C DATE SIGNED	28D PHYSICIAN'S LICENSE NUMBER
	28E TYPE PHYSICIAN'S NAME AND ADDRESS		

INJURY INFORMATION

29 SPECIFY ACCIDENT, SUICIDE, ETC.	30 PLACE OF INJURY	31 INJURY AT WORK	32A DATE OF INJURY — MONTH, DAY, YEAR	32B HOUR
Pending				

33 LOCATION (STREET AND NUMBER OR LOCATION AND CITY OR TOWN)	34 DESCRIBE HOW INJURY OCCURRED (EVENTS WHICH RESULTED IN INJURY)

CORONER'S USE ONLY

35A I CERTIFY THAT DEATH OCCURRED AT THE HOUR, DATE AND PLACE STATED FROM THE CAUSES STATED, AS REQUIRED BY LAW, I HAVE HELD AN INQUEST-INVESTIGATION	35B CORONER SIGNATURE AND DEGREE OR TITLE Raymond L. Carrillo, Coroner By: Nancy Grower, Deputy	35C DATE SIGNED 02-06-87
Investigation		

36 DISPOSITION	37 DATE — MONTH, DAY, YEAR	38 NAME AND ADDRESS OF CEMETERY OR CREMATORY	39 EMBALMER'S LICENSE NUMBER AND SIGNATURE
Entombment	February 7, 1987	Forest Lawn Memorial- Park, 6300 Forest Lawn Drive, Los Angeles, Cal. 762	

40A NAME OF FUNERAL DIRECTOR (OR PERSON ACTING AS SUCH)	40B LICENSE NO.	41 LOCAL REGISTRAR SIGNATURE	42 DATE ACCEPTED BY LOCAL REGISTRAR
Forest Lawn Hollywood Hills Mty.	F-904		February 6, 1987

STATE	A.	B.	C.	D.	E.	F.